Quick Wisdom

Professional guide

By Marriage and Family Therapist

Abe Kass MA RSW RMFT CCHT

The 15 Essential Facts

Victims of Emotional Abuse

Need to Know

I hope you are not living your life as an abused individual. Chronic emotional abuse is an emotional pain that does not go away. The injuries caused by abuse, depending on the severity and length of time over which they have occurred, can be severe.

Emotional abuse is a crime in every meaning of the word. If emotional or psychological abuse describes your relationship with your partner, I implore you to do something to change your situation. To allow abuse to continue is absolutely unacceptable.

Initially, your greatest weapon to stop the abuse is "knowledge." You need to know what is happening to you, understand it, and have words to describe it. You need that for your own sanity and also to be able to reach out and get help from others. This book is dedicated to giving you the knowledge you need to — know what you need to know — to stop the abuse.

It is not easy to determine if you are emotionally abused or psychologically abused. Emotional abuse and psychological abuse do not leave cuts, wounds or broken bones like physical abuse or domestic violence.

(If you are a victim of physical abuse and domestic violence see the links at the bottom of this page for helpful links. If you are in immediate danger, call the police.)

If you are a victim of emotional abuse or psychological abuse, your fear, confusion, and brainwashing may make it difficult for you to recognize that you are an emotionally abused man or emotionally abused woman who lives in an emotional abusive relationship.

Unlike a physically abusive relationship, emotional and psychological abuse leaves no marks on the body. Because emotional abuse and psychological abuse are often hidden, this is why it is important that you study the points in this book that will describe the characteristics of an emotionally abusive marriage or committed relationship. You need to look deeper to understand what is happening to you.

This book, **The 15 Essential Facts Victims of Emotional Abuse Need to Know** will cover all the various aspects of emotional abuse. You can use this book as a guide to help you determine your status, and if you conclude, you are being abused, what your options are — what you can do about being emotionally or psychologically abused.

Allowing the abuse you are suffering from and being injured by to 'just continue' should not be an option. Rather, you need to take decisive actions to stop this cruelty. But first, before you can choose the right path for you, you need to arm yourself with "knowledge."

Note: To date, researchers have not made a clear distinction between emotional abuse and psychological abuse. Thus, I use the two words interchangeably.

Learn more if you are in a physically abusive relationship: https://www.gosmartlife.com/physical-abuse-violence

Fact #1: Abuse comes in 5 different forms

There are 5 categories of abuse:

Individuals seek different things in life and have aptitudes in different areas of life. So too, with abusive partners. Some are more interested in humiliating their partner, some controlling their partner, and some enslaving their partner. So too, some abusers are skilled with their tongue and others with their hands. All these variations contribute to the following 5 general categories of abuse.

1. **Emotional and psychological abuse**

Emotional and psychological abuse is characterized by challenging your very thought process, self-worth, and core values.

Emotional and psychological abuse is a form of mind control similar to the brainwashing used by cults.

Emotional and psychological abuse is characterized by telling you that what you want is wrong, how you think is wrong, and that being independent is wrong.

All threats that make you feel insecure, worthless, and trapped are variations of emotion and psychological abuse.

In the extreme, persistent emotional and psychological abuse can cause the victim to lose all objectivity about the realities of life and lead to feelings of "being crazy and out of control."

2. **Verbal abuse**

Verbal abuse is directives and opinions by the abuser expressed to the victim with harsh and cruel words.

You may be told that you are stupid, ugly, or hopeless. These are all ways — and many other variances of these words — to hurt your feelings, make you feel bad, and ultimately to force you into subservience.

Verbal abuse will eventually erode your self-esteem and lead to anxiety and depression. If you are a victim of verbal abuse, your relationship has or will crash leaving you uncomfortable in the presence of your partner.

3. **Physical abuse and domestic violence**

Physical abuse and domestic violence is violent assault and a crime.

Physical abuse and domestic violence define the character of the relationship — which is that the abuser has the right to indiscriminately use physical violence and confiscate valued and necessary items in order to impose his or her will through fear, torture, and pain.

Your abuser may hit you, push you, kick you or throw things at you — this is physical abuse. Physical abuse is not defined by an injury. Rather, physical abuse is the use of brute force to impose his or her will upon a victim regardless of whether or not there is an injury.

As well, physical abuse includes locking you out of the house, confiscating your belongings, or confining you by restricting your movement.

Physical abuse and domestic violence are dangerous and completely unacceptable.

Physical abuse and domestic violence that is ongoing

is repugnant. It undermines the very purpose as to why two individuals choose to join together and form a family.

If you are being physically abused and danger is imminent, call the police. Get long-term help by reaching out to the authorities and mental health professionals.

4. Sexual abuse

Sexual activity between committed individuals must be consensual and pleasurable for each person. When sex is forced upon an unwilling partner, it is sexual abuse.

If you feel compelled to engage in sexual activity with your partner out of fear for your emotional or physical safety, this then is sexual abuse. The right to determine what happens with your body is a fundamental basic human right. Sexual abuse violates this human right and violates your dignity and human entitlement to self-determination.

5. Spiritual and doctrine abuse

Some individuals use scripture and other doctrines to

force their partner to behave in certain ways.

For example, the abuser threatens his or her partner that if a particular ritual or procedure is not followed, then damnation will follow or severe punishment will come to members of the family.

In spiritual abuse, the abuser takes the position that he or she is the beholder of privileged knowledge or has a special relationship with a Higher Power that then entitles him or her to control his or her partner.

Typically, the victim of spiritual or doctrine abuse is fearful, lacks self-confidence, and feels humiliated all in the name of God or some other "ism" such as communism.

It is not possible to compare the various types of abuse and determine which is worse. Any one of them can lead to very harmful consequences. As well, each person has a different way of experiencing abuse.

Having said that, clearly physical abuse and domestic violence can lead to death. Over the years, thousands upon thousands of people have died at the hands of their hostile and aggressive partners.

Death is something that cannot be reversed; there is no recovery. Every type of abuse can slip into a final act that can in a brief moment snuff out a person's life. Without saying which abuse is worse, we can unequivocally say all abuse is wrong, unacceptable, and must stop.

All forms of abuse are wrong; no one has a right to control or cause pain to another.

If you are being abused — no matter what form it is in — you need to find a way to make it stop.

Fact #2: The 5 ways emotional abuse destroys relationships

As cancer is to the body... emotional abuse is to marriages and committed relationships.

Emotional abuse over time will erode your relationship taking it from one of love, closeness, and trust to one of fear, resentment, and horror.

If the problem of emotional abuse cannot be solved there is really only one reasonable solution, to terminate the relationship. That is, if you want to maintain your emotional health, safety, and sanity! However, terminating your relationship is not always necessary.

Fortunately, there is much you can do to stop emotional abuse; reasonable and practical solutions can be found. This is why I have written this book.

First, you are going to learn how to identify emotional or psychological abuse and towards the end of this book, you will be presented with various options to stop the abuse you are suffering from.

This topic — emotional abuse — is personal to you, and it should be. Like high blood pressure, emotional abuse should not be ignored. Like high blood pressure which is described as a "silent killer," emotional abuse can kill all the good in your marriage or committed relationship and destroy you, and if you have children, them as well. Don't ignore it!

Let's now discuss some of the reasons emotional abuse is so damaging to relationships and individuals in an emotionally abusive relationship.

The 5 ways emotional abuse destroys relationships

Safety, Trust, Friendship, Love, and Intimacy, are 5 necessary ingredients in a healthy, happy, and long-lasting relationship, all are destroyed by emotional or psychological abuse. Here how:

1. **Safety**

The cornerstone of every healthy relationship is feeling safe when you are with your partner or when you anticipate his or her presence.

Sadly, feeling safe in an abusive relationship is not

possible. Being put down, criticized, insulted, threatened, and more are the weapons that are used to coerce the victim of abuse. Under such circumstances, how is it possible to feel safe?

Underlying most manifestations of abuse is anger. Anger evokes in its recipient fear. Fear and feeling unsafe go 'hand and hand.'

Anger is expressed in many different ways. It can be bombastic and aggressive, or it can be hidden in sarcastic jokes or refusals to talk and everything in between. Most relationships, including those that cannot be categorized as "abusive," deteriorate because of anger.

As a victim of abuse, fear of your abuser has seized your mind and left you mentally paralyzed when in the presence of your abuser. Likely you fear his coming home from work; her critical comments; his threats; her rejection. It is understandable why you feel unsafe while at the same time you feel trapped not knowing how to avoid these crushing feelings.

Your relationship at one time was loving, and it has now turned from a feel-good experience to one of discomfort and emotional pain.

Each human being is entitled to live in safety. Safety is not something that requires effort or meritorious behavior. It is a human right; a God given right — and we are all entitled to it freely and unconditionally.

When you anticipate emotional pain knowing that your partner will be present shortly, when you experience emotional pain, you will feel unsafe. This is normal, and this is because your partner has abused you and continues to do so.

Feeling unsafe in an abusive relationship is a given.

Solve your emotional abuse problem, and you can once again feel safe!

2. **Trust**

Trust is necessary for every healthy and successful relationship. However, if someone hurts you repeatedly and shows no remorse... how can you trust them?

Relentless emotional attacks without remorse is an everyday occurrence in an emotionally abusive relationship.

When somebody disrespects you, criticizes you, disregards your feelings, how can you trust them?

How can you trust someone who has so little regard for your well-being?

Answer: *Such a person you cannot trust!*

Trust is sacrificed when there is emotional abuse. *Trust is returned when the emotional abuse ceases.*

3. **Friendship**

Friendship is for those couples who are loving, caring and respectful with each other... abusive relationships have none of these qualities.

Who wants to be around a person who makes another feel bad? Not you and not I!

To achieve his or her purpose to dominate and control, abusers have many tools that hurt and intimidate all of which destroys friendship.

If your partner causes you pain, you will not be his or her friend.

Even children know to avoid mean classmates! If your partner is repeatedly hurting you, you will certainly not consider him or her a friend. Enemy yes, friend no!

Healthy relationships exist precisely because two individuals feel a camaraderie with each other — a friendship. They want to be with each other, share with each other, play with each other, and grow together. An emotionally abusive relationship has none of this — it is the opposite of a healthy relationship.

Friendship and emotional abuse are mutual exclusives! Stop the abuse and let "friendship" return!

4. **Love**

Forget about it! If you are being abused, there can be no love.

Emotional abuse is bad relationship chemistry!

If the abuse ends, over time it is possible to recover the love... maybe? The mind has a talent at holding on to negative memories. It is possible to recover from emotional abuse, but it is not given.

Love is like a delicate flower. Taking good care of love is the best way to ensure it stays beautiful and sweet.

If emotional abuse has caused your love to wither, know that you are running out of time to solve your abuse problem before it becomes too late to change things around. Once an egg falls and smashes, it can never be put together again — often the same is true for love.

If the abuse stops and you choose to stay together, you may sadly have to settle for a marriage of convenience. Staying together may be worth it, but your marriage will never have the purity and passion it once had.

The sooner you can solve your emotional abuse problem, the sooner you can get to work to see if you can rekindle the love you once had.

5. Intimacy

Relationship intimacy is the sharing of the most private parts of an individual with another individual.

Healthy relationships have a sanctity precisely

because of the intimacy — the privacy that is not shared with anyone else other than one's partner.

This is why for example, infidelity is so devastating to the betrayed partner. The intimacy that is intrinsic in the committed relationship has been violated. Emotional abuse so too violates intimacy in many ways since the privacy is used as another means to hurt one's partner rather than build safety, trust, friendship, and love.

Intimacy is the fruit born of Safety, Trust, Friendship, and Love. When these relationship nutrients are missing... there cannot be intimacy — only a forced bonding that is detested and resented by both parties.

You cannot open up — sexually, emotionally, intellectually, or spiritually — when your relationship is marred by fear and disrespect.

Sadly, it is possible that your abusive partner does not realize that he or she has killed the intimacy between the two of you precisely because of his or her bad behavior.

Intimacy is for those individuals who are blessed to

be in a healthy and happy relationship. If your marriage or a committed relationship is marred by abuse, there will be no intimacy, and likely your marriage will be sexless — unless sex is being forced which in this case is another form of abuse and is an additional assault upon your relationship.

For many couples, — especially young ones — sexual love is the greatest form of intimacy. It is also the greatest casualty of a relationship that is emotionally or psychologically destroyed by abusive.

If you are to have a healthy and satisfying sexual love-life, you need to have a healthy and satisfying emotional relationship that includes safety, trust, friendship, and love.

With your partner of choice, intimacy is the goal and abuse is the obstacle. Remove the abuse, and intimacy has an opportunity to take root, grow, and over time blossom.

Fact #3: There are 14 definitive signs of emotionally abusive behavior

Emotional abuse can be categorized by 14 types of identifying beliefs and their accompanying behavior.

The descriptions of these 14 types of abusive behavior have evolved out of my clinical experience working with hundreds of individuals living in abusive relationships and my research into domestic abuse.

However, each actual 'abusive interaction' typically includes more than one type of abusive behavior. The lines between the various types of abusive behavior are to some extent arbitrary.

For example, a wife tells her husband he is "sick in the head" for wanting to play poker with his friends then hides the keys to his car so he can't leave their house. She then blocks his way to the bedroom when he attempts to get his spare car key while threatening to call the police and accuse him of assault. This single abusive act includes emotional abuse /

psychological abuse, verbal abuse, and physical abuse / domestic violence.

Each of the following 14 acts of abusive behavior has a component of emotional abuse, and each manifestation is wrong and unacceptable.

Emotional abuse is primarily characterized by the perpetrator of abuse using emotional manipulation and assault as a means to control his or her victim.

Your abuser achieves his or her purpose with harsh criticisms, threats, pointing out past mistakes, criticizing your birth family and friends. And this is not enough, all of this expressed with extreme anger. The abuser's goal is to make you feel like a bad and worthless person.

The emotional abuser intends to break the spirit of his or her partner. Achieving this gives the abuser a false sense of security. The abuser feels that now that his or her partner has been weakened, he or she cannot challenge his or her desires, point out mistakes, or leave the relationship.

The abuser achieves a "false sense of security" because in reality he or she has created a horrible relationship that is unstable by the very fact that his or her partner naturally wants to avoid him or her or to leave the relationship and will do so should it become possible.

Your abuser may have grown-up in a family where those types of emotional manipulations were commonplace. He or she may not even realize the full extent of how wrong and harmful it is using emotional abusive behavior to make you feel bad so you can be more easily dominated.

Emotional abuse as described above, if allowed to go unchecked, will destroy your self-esteem and eliminate your happiness and feelings of security.

14 acts of abusive behavior

Read each item, pause, think and decide if the following intents and behaviors describe your relationship. Each one of the following 14 behavioral acts are examples of emotionally abusive behavior.

1. **Aggressive behavior with the intent to control.**

Not all fighting in a marriage is emotional abuse.

Emotionally abusive relationships are characterized by the abuser having an "intent" to dominate his or her partner.

All emotionally abusive relationships have the clear intention and purpose to humiliate, dominate, shame, and control another person.

For example, when Donald warns his wife Sharon that she must be ready when he wants to leave for their trip, otherwise there will be negative "consequences," he intends to teach her to be obedient and to recognize his authority. Donald is training his wife to comply with his wishes which include "being ready on time," which includes his ultimate goal that Sharon follows every one of his directives. *This is emotionally abuse behavior.*

2. A belief that "might makes right."

Abusers use their 'imposed authority' to control their victims. Believing that a strong person can control the relationship, the abuser breaks the will of his or her victim to establish his or her dominance. Once the abuser's dominance has been established, it can readily be used to impose total control of his or her partner.

For example, Michael controls all the money in his family and only gives his committed partner Susan what he feels is "reasonable." Susan is not working so she has no money of her own. Michael believes that since he is the wage earner in the family, this gives him the 'right' to control how money is spent. Michael believes that Susan's opinion on how to use their financial resources simply does not matter. *This is emotionally abuse behavior.*

3. **A willingness to escalate the conflict.**

An abusive person is prepared to go as far as necessary to establish his or her dominance — normal social limits do not apply. The abusive person may take away his or her partner's car keys, threaten to take away the children, assert that his or her partner is "crazy" and will be committed to a psychiatric ward and use other psychologically abusive mind control games. The abuser's intent is to weaken his or her partner so he or she can be easily dominated.

For example, Tina threatened her husband Tom that if

he doesn't help her with chores around the house she will leave him and he will then lose his contact with the children. *This is emotionally abuse behavior.*

4. **Duration of the conflict.**

An abusive person is persistent and does not let go of what he or she wants until his or her will has been achieved. It is this dogged determination that shows the true intent of the abuser which is to dominate and control.

For example, Karen would wake her husband Eric in the middle of the night and repeatedly tell him how disappointed she was in his behavior as a father. These attacks often went on for hours and were repeated for several consecutive nights. *This is emotionally abuse behavior.*

5. **Willingness to maintain the conflict.**

An abusive person is ruthless in his or her efforts to dominate and maintain control. Repetitive themes such as the victim 'spends too much money,' is 'interested in other people' outside the marriage, 'talks to his or her parents too much,' and the like are used to erode the victim's sense of security and confidence making him or her easy prey for domination.

For example, Tony can be irritable. During dinner, he snapped at Sean, his thirteen-year-old son, and ordered him to put away his phone. Tony's wife, Melinda immediately chastised him for his disciplining Sean. In the presence of the three children, Melinda continued to ream out her husband, Tony. Later in that evening she brought up his disciplining Sean again and told him what a bad father he was. Finally, when Tony got to sleep at 12 o'clock he was then awoken an hour later by Melinda who continued to berate him for being a "bad father." The next day, Melinda sent Tony a barrage of text messages insisting he take a Parenting Class. Melinda was relentless in her attacks on Tony. *This is emotionally abuse behavior.*

6. **Tyranny.**

Threats, intimidation, bodily harm, treating one's partner as an object to be manipulated, opposing the rights of a partner to assert his or her will and the need to establish control is obvious emotional abuse.

For example, Tim was a successful lawyer. His clients paid top dollar to get his advice about how to solve their legal matters, and his secretaries did his bidding. When Tim came home, he made it clear to his wife that she was to follow his directives. She was not to question him, oppose him, or negotiate with him. If she did, Tim would respond with threats to divorce her, threats to take away the children, threats to tell people what a horrible person she was, and to abandon her and leave her destitute. *This is emotionally abuse behavior.*

7. **Not caring for others.**

Neglect of the legitimate needs of others and his or her obligations to care for his or her partner is emotional abuse. So too, is being indifferent to a partner's emotional, physical, spiritual or medical needs is emotional abuse.

For example, Sam had been diagnosed with a neurological disorder. Over time, he lost his mobility and became confined to a wheelchair. His wife Amanda would not accept her husband in this compromised state of being. She neglected his every need. She withdrew her care and abandoned him to his own resources which were limited due to his lack of mobility. Often, after work instead of going home and attending to the needs of her husband Sam, Amanda would go out with coworkers to enjoy the evenings in restaurants and bars. Sam's medical needs were only attended to by the hired dayworker. Amanda had no interest in what Sam's doctor said and his prognosis. Eventually, Sam discovered his wife was committing adultery. *This is emotionally abuse behavior.*

8. **Unaccountable.**

An emotionally abusive partner rejects taking responsibility for psychologically or physically harming his or her partner. An abusive partner ignores social rules, authority, and rectifying his or her past mistakes.

For example, Charlie loves fast cars. As well, Charlie loves alcohol. Often he would combine the two. Maria, his wife, pleaded with him not to drink and drive, but to no avail. Charlie just 'blew her off' and continued doing what he loved. He was reckless, and whenever Maria was in the car with him, he ignored her pleas to slow down. She was frightened and controlled by his domination. Worst of all, even when the children were in the vehicle, it made no difference to Charlie. Marie's pleas to her husband to act safely and responsibly fell on deaf ears. Once Charlie crashed into a highway barrier. Fortunately, no one was injured. When Marie claimed the accident was caused by Charlie's speeding and drinking, he turned it around and blamed her for the accident claiming she nagged him so much that this caused him to become distracted which then led to the accident. *This is emotionally abuse behavior.*

9. **Dictatorship.**

Unilateral decision making, secrecy, deceptive communication, unresponsive to the impact his or her decisions have on others is emotional abuse.

For example, Harry did not like his job. His solution was simple. He went and got another job in a different state. Without any discussion, he uprooted his wife and their two children and relocated them without considering their needs. Margaret, Harry's wife, left behind her aging parents and her three siblings. Adjusting to life in a new place was daunting, and she felt guilty leaving her parents.

Within a few months, Margaret became depressed. Harry responded to Margaret's difficulties by claiming she was not supportive. *This is emotionally abuse behavior.*

10. **Insensitive to the needs of others.**

Not caring about the individual needs, feelings, and opinions of other family members, and seeing others as objects or placeholders to be positioned for the benefit of the abuser is emotionally abusive behavior.

For example, Chantel decided one day to become a vegetarian. Her husband Mark wanted to eat a traditional Western diet which included meat. Without any discussion or consensus, Chantel stopped cooking meat and instead prepared complex vegetarian meals. Mark protested and explained that this "new food" gave him stomach aches and made it difficult for him to sleep at night. Chantel responded telling Mark that eating meat was unhealthy and that she didn't want it and would not cook or serve it. Rather, Chantel asserted her "right" to cook whatever she wanted, and if he didn't like it, he could go to a restaurant to eat. *This is emotionally abuse behavior.*

11. **Excessive autonomy.**

The abuser makes no commitment to others and does not acknowledge his or her obligations and responsibilities as a senior member of the family. The abusive person is not willing to integrate strengths and vulnerabilities to form a team.

For example, Jacqueline was pregnant. She felt nausea, had difficulty bending over and lifting heavy objects. All of this made no difference to her husband, Peter. Whatever her responsibilities were before pregnancy, in his mind, they were the same now. He would not help her bring in the groceries from the car or pick up anything from the floor. According to Peter, her pregnancy problems where her "problems" — not his. *This is emotionally abuse behavior.*

12. **Harsh judgments.**

The abuser has no empathy, compassion, and support during loss, distress, illness and emotional pain.

For example, Andy lost his job. Now in his late 50s, it is difficult to find a new one. His wife, Dawn, has no compassion for him. She demands that he provide her with money and is indifferent to the fact that he is depressed and anxious. Her attitude is that she should not be inconvenienced because her husband of 25 years is now unemployed. *This is emotionally abuse behavior.*

13. Extreme selfishness.

The abusive person feels entitled to have everything his or her way. The abuser does not credit the contributions his or her partner makes to the family. And since the abuser is entitled to "everything," he or she sees no reason to ever compromise with anyone.

Kurt loves sports; he loves playing, going to sports events, and he loves watching sports on TV. Everyone in the family has to accommodate Kurt's "love of sports." When it is a Sunday, no one was allowed in the family-room while Kurt watches a sports event. He is indifferent to his wife's pleas that he participate in family activities. Simply, Kurt tells her that at he works hard all week and he is entitled to relax and that everyone else should just get a life and leave him alone. *This is emotionally abuse behavior.*

14. **Rejecting.**

The abusive person does not accept the individual needs of others, the flexible application of rules and agreements, and is unwilling to accept the legitimate limitations of others.

For example, Thomas has agreed to give the children baths nightly. Sharon, his wife, appreciates Thomas's help with the children. One of Thomas's friends had exclusive box seat tickets to a major sporting event. Attending the sporting event meant that Thomas would miss one night helping Sharon with the children. Sharon rejected Thomas's request to be excused for the special sporting event. Thomas tried to reason with Sharon and proposed that he would take care of the children alone for a few nights and she could take the time to go out with her friends. Sharon rejected all of her husband's request and proposed compromise and insisted that he be home and miss the sporting event. She threatened that if he went to the sport event she would leave with the children and he would be left alone. *This is emotionally abuse behavior.*

Even one of the above signs of emotional abuse IS

abuse. A person does not need more than one tumor to have cancer...one is enough! So too with abuse. Any one of the above signs, if it exists in your relationship should not be allowed to continue.

The only difference between one abusive behavior and many abusive behaviors is that that the fewer there are, likely the easier it is to stop; to completely eliminate it from your relationship. As an analogy, it is easier to master one chapter in a technical book than many. So too, the 'less change' that is required to transform your relationship to one of respect, sensitivity, and care, the easier it will be.

If you conclude you are in an emotionally abusive marriage or committed relationship, you need to take clear and decisive action to stop the abuse. This will be further discussed below.

Know, like a virus, emotional abuse spreads to everyone in the family — the perpetrator of emotional abuse, the victim of emotional abuse and if there are children in your family, they too suffer and are hurt.

Don't think, "I will take the abuse to keep the family together." Regardless of what you think — if you are abused... your children are hurt.

Emotional abuse is a serious matter!

Fact #4: Not all relationship fighting is abuse

Relationships can be very healthy and positive and still occasionally be stressed by verbal bickering, arguing and fighting.

Your marriage or committed relationship may experience the occasional argument, insensitivity, selfishness or expressions of anger. This does not mean you are in an abusive relationship. It also does not mean that you should just accept arguments as a normal part of marriage. Yes, it happens—but it doesn't have to.

You should work on your relationship and get to the point where peace and harmony reign always or almost always... this should be your goal.

Emotional abuse it is characterized by a systemic and unending disrespect and effort to control, combined with a total disregard for the wellbeing of his or her partner.

The abusive person never apologizes because he or

she feels it is his or her right control. The abusive person may exonerate him or herself, claiming you are a loser and he or she must take control. Don't buy into this nonsense. No one has a right to control you or anyone else!

If there is occasional fighting, or even if it is more common than occasional, this means you are in a difficult marriage. However, when the fighting is an effort to erode your self-worth and diminish your legitimate entitlements to self-determination, this is abuse.

A "difficult marriage" is characterized by efforts to determine the outcome of a particular issue. An "emotionally abusive marriage" is characterized by the abuser seeking to diminish the worth of his or her partner and establish dominance.

Here are 3 tips to improve 'any type' of marriage

1. Have realistic expectations

When "expectations" are unrealistic — frustration and disappointment is imminent. When expectations are balanced and realistic, it is relatively easy to feel content.

It is essential to marital contentment that expectations are aligned with one's partner's aptitude. "He may never be the best communicator, but it is ok." "She may never be well organized and tidy, but I can live with it." Adjusting one's "expectations" to the reality of one's partner is good marriage advice and contributes directly to relationship harmony.

As well, all successful couples and families must adapt to changing circumstances. Be they changes that are predictable like the birth of children or advancing age, or changes that are unanticipated such as unemployment or serious illness. All these challenges require an adjustment of one's expectations.

The best marriage help is often simply maintaining "low expectations" about what your partner can and cannot do for you.

2. Communication

Satisfying conversations between a husband and

wife build closeness and trust.

Marital research has shown that there needs to be at least 5 positive interactions to each negative one for there to be feelings of closeness. Even one criticism, or angry outburst, can undo the value of many positive interactions. (The mind remembers negative interactions longer than positive ones!)

Understanding this highlights the importance of continually engaging in positive and pleasant communication, while trying to minimize negative interactions. The challenge is to produce the greatest number of positive verbal interactions with the fewest negative interactions.

If your relationship is in serious trouble, pleasant interactions alone may be able to save your marriage and prevent divorce.

3. Conflict resolution

The goal in marriage is to live together in peace and harmony. However, for many couples, marriage will at times include occasional disagreements or conflicts. When this happens, it is essential to keep the conflict small and contained.

Successful conflict resolution requires 3 criteria:

1. **Stay respectful:** No name calling, expressions of strong anger, bulling, or attempts to humiliate.

2. **Stick to one topic:** Stay focused exclusively on the issue at hand. Resist dragging into the conversation other areas of disagreement or disappointment.

3. **Keep it small:** The disagreement should only last a few minutes and then be quickly set aside, and efforts should be made to restore positive feelings and constructive interactions.

Unlike what many believe, relationship harmony is not "chemistry," — rather its hard work leading to concrete relationship skills.

Marriage research shows that couples that score high in these three areas, although not necessarily perfect in every way, share happy and meaningful lives.

Fact #5: Expressing anger kills relationships

One of the most pronounced characteristics of emotional abuse is the abundant use of anger to hurt, shame, frighten, bully, and humiliate.

Typically, anger is the weapon of choice for most abusers. As murderers have guns that shoot bullets, emotional abusers have a mouth that shoots angry critical words.

Standing-up to a bully is easier said than done! Your abuser knows all of this and uses it to her advantage.

As humans, we have a visceral reaction to anger. We are naturally inclined to seek ways to make it stop. In the moment, complying with what the angry person wants seems to be the easy way out. However, in most cases it is not.

When you give in to an angry person, that emboldens him or her to continue to use anger in the future to control you. Compliance with what the angry person wants unintentionally rewards anger and increases the likelihood it will then be used in the future. Surrendering to anger is not a reasonable plan for stopping abuse.

There are many additional ways an abuser imposes his or her control. Passive-aggressive behavior, rejection, threats of catastrophic punishments, name-calling, and shaming are just a few. *However, anger tops the list as the most used instrument of abuse.*

If you are to solve your emotional abuse problems in your relationship, then the abusive person needs to learn how to control his or her anger and stay calm and respectful.

Here are 5 anger management tips to help you and your partner stay calm

1. **Resist negatively judging your partner.** Seek positive ways to interpret your partner's behavior, so you will be less upset or not upset at all with what he or she has done.

2. **Don't keep a score.** When you are upset with something your partner has done, "forgive and forget." Don't hold on to your negative judgment

about your partner and angry feelings and use them as fuel to feed additional negative thoughts. This will only lead to additional anger and escalated conflict — you and your entire family will then suffer the consequences.

3. **Be humble.** Don't react in an angry way when things don't go your way. In essence, anger is trying to force things to be different than they are. Anger is an aggressive emotion to try and "force" things to be the way you want them to be. Whatever the situation is, try to accept as much as you can. "Acceptance" will eliminate anger and this will lead to peace and harmony with your partner.

4. **Share and Negotiate.** If there is something your partner does that you cannot "accept" as recommended above — and perhaps for a good reason — calmly and respectfully share your thoughts and when appropriate, negotiate a solution agreeable to both of you.

5. **Stay calm.** If you become angry, stop talking. Do something else until you calm down. When you are angry everyone around you is hurt including you, and the point you are trying to make is lost in the flood of

negative emotions. *Only try to explain yourself or get what you want when you are calm!*

When you follow these anger prevention guidelines, this will be a miraculous tonic to improve the peace and harmony in every relationship.

Fact #6. Emotional abuse is a two-way street — both men and women can be abused

A man can abuse a woman, and a woman can abuse a man. In my marriage therapy practice, I have encountered both scenarios.

However, men are naturally more aggressive, possessive and competitive and thus can slip into being abusive more easily than women.

As well, society teaches boys and men that they are entitled to dominate women and women are taught to serve men. Being "macho," for some men is a sign of being 'cool,' although it is not. And some women think, "serving" men is their duty.

Thus, some men don't even realize they are behaving abusively. They think behaving aggressively and controlling is part of their entitlement as a man. Such men, if they are to succeed in their relationships with their female partners need to learn that all abuse is wrong and they must stop their bad behavior. And some women allow abuse to part of their relationship, thinking it is their responsibility to accept a dominating and mean-spirited partner. Such women need to learn that they are equal to men and entitled to a full degree of respect, sensitivity, and consideration.

When a woman abuses a man it is often difficult to notice. A woman's abuse is a more quiet and sustained. As well, people do not expect women to be abusive and therefore it is often overlooked or underestimated. On the other hand, in some cases men of bad character who are not really abusive, are none the less seen as being an abuser because people expect men to be that way.Sometimes, a trained relationship specialist is needed to help evaluate the intent of an individual to determine if the behavior in question is a manifestation of bad character or is abuse for the purpose of controlling one's partner.

There is no legitimate excuse for abuse — be it from a man or be it from a woman.

Fact #7. Abuse is not your fault

If you are a victim of abuse, know that it is never your fault. No matter how you explain your circumstances, being abused is inexcusable and never deserved or warranted.

In a family setting, no person has a right to hurt another person. The person abusing you is wrong... *plain and simple!*

"Respect and kindness" are not a prize for good behavior — it is a human right!

The person abusing you may say you deserve his or her cruel and insensitive treatment, but his words are false, do not believe them. It is your abuser and not you who is out of line.

No one is perfect and no one deserves to be abused!

Know the truth and stick stubbornly to it in every situation and at all times!

Fact #8. Don't keep your abuse a secret — talk to others

Many people who are abused feel ashamed falsely believing that somehow the abuse is their fault; that they are to blame. Because of these feelings, they hide their abuse from others. Unfortunately, doing so only makes their situation worse and more difficult to resolve.

Keeping your abuse secret will distract you from what you really need to do which is to get help to improve your situation; to eliminate the abuse and if possible to reestablish respect and kindness in your relationship and if not to leave your abusive partner.

You can't do it alone

Coping with and exiting out of abuse often requires the help of others. You need to reach out and trust that others will be there for you — and in most cases they will be.

Others can help you make sure your exit is safe or if you stay how to eliminate the abuse. They can help you get the resources you need. And they can encourage you as you travel the long and hard road ahead to freedom.

Your "helpers" do not need to be perfect

Those that will help you are not always going to have all the answers. Sometimes they may be overemotional and thus overreact. However, they are part of a bigger plan to encourage you to take the action needed to free yourself from your unacceptable situation.

A team approach is often best

The individuals you gather around to assist will be unique to your own needs. The following are a list of some common helpers who may or may not be useful to you:

- Police

- Psychologists, Social workers, Counselors

- Lawyers

- Support groups

- Child welfare agencies

- Hospital agencies

- Women's shelters

If someone needs an operation, there will be an entire team of specialized health professions to successfully complete the job. So too, solving your abusive situation may require a team of professionals, family members, and friends. You will likely need several different types of individuals to assist and help you complete the needed tasks to establish a life of respect and dignity.

Fact #9. You are entitled to respect — The 10 characteristics of respect

Respect and dignity are a God given right, or if you prefer, a human right.

You DO NOT need to "earn" respect. You DO NOT need special status to live with dignity. Anyone who interferes with your right to "respect and dignity" is certainly committing a moral crime and in some cases a legal crime as well.

The bottom line — respect and dignity are an intrinsic part of life itself. Just as you have a right to breathe, make decisions, and to live in freedom... so too you have a right to be treated by others with respect and dignity.

You chose a partner to love and care for you and so you too can do the same for him or her. To be abused by the very person you have chosen to share your life with is the ultimate relationship perversion and should not be tolerated!

Note that every individual occasionally slips and disrespects his or her partner. *This does not constitute abuse.* There is a significant difference between being abused and needing a marital tune-up.

Abuse is the systematic effort to break down the victim's sense of worth. To bend her will to his; to force him to do her bidding. Keep this point in mind as you compare the following relationship dynamics to your own marriage or committed relationship.

10 Relationship characteristics of respect

1. **When your partner treats you like an adult.** You and your partner may have very different ideas on many different things. However, your point of view and way of doing things should be viewed as valid. (There are occasional exceptions when a person's point of view is unreasonable. However, for most people these "unreasonable moments" are rare.)

For example: Tom wanted to buy a new car for himself. Winter was coming and he didn't want to risk being late for work because the old car was unreliable. So he spoke to his wife Susan and shared

53

his feelings about getting a new car. Together they made a decision to postpone buying a car until the following year. *This is respect.*

When your partner treats you like a child — this is disrespect and if it happens often it is emotional abuse

Marriage is the joining together of two equal people. Anything less is perverse and is a failure in the relationship.

For example: Mary wanted to go to her parent's cottage for a barbecue. Dan wanted to stay home explaining that he needed some downtime. Mary told him he was being silly not understanding how important her parents were to her. She told him to "grow-up" and act like a man. *This is disrespect.*

2. **To have positive regard for you.** Your partner needs to view you as a good person even if your way of doing things may be different than his or hers.

For example: Sharon thinks highly of her husband. It is easy for her to express her gratitude and appreciation for all he does. It comes naturally to her and he senses her positive regard. *This is respect.*

To see you as inadequate — this is disrespect and if it happens often it is emotional abuse

If your partner thinks you are a loser, a fool or stupid, etc., this will eventually lead to a relationship characterized by disrespect.

For example, Philip sees his wife as weak and inept. He always tells her how to do everything including how to slice a tomato. Susan feels disrespected, and it is understandable why! *This is disrespect.*

3. **To be sensitive to your feelings.** To be sensitive to your feelings means to be aware and take into consideration how what he or she wants will effect you. Because how you feel is important, decisions are shared.

For example: Sharron intended to go and visit her elderly mother who lived out of town. She wanted to stay a few extra days to visit old friends. Since her husband, Sam would be caring for the kids, she asked him how he felt about her being away from the family for an extended period of time. *This is respect.*

To disregard your feelings — this is disrespect and if it happens often it is emotional abuse

To be unwilling to consult with you or listen to you regarding what you want is a characteristic of emotional abuse.

For example, Tony automatically responds that he's busy whenever his wife Karen wants to speak with him. His being busy is "the rule" and not the exception. *This is disrespect.*

4. **Agreeing you have equal rights.** No person has a right to dominate over another. You and your partner may be different. You may have talent in one area and he or she in another. Regardless, you are both equal in value and entitled to equal rights.

For example: Eric told his wife Kim that did not want to hear a local politician speak. However, he told Kim that if she wanted to go, he was fine with that. He suggested she might like to go with a friend. *This is respect.*

To refuse to acknowledge your rights — this is disrespect and if it happens often it is emotional abuse

You have a right to pursue happiness, be free and to make decisions. If your partner stands in the way of these rights and tries to prevent you from executing them, this is abuse.

For example: Before John was married he was an active athlete. He had many friends and a full social life.

After the wedding, his wife Amy insisted he stay with her whenever he wasn't at work. She would go into a rage and throw things when John attempted to spend time with his friends or to participate in a sports activity. Amy did not acknowledge John's right to be happy and make decisions. *This is disrespect.*

5. **To only touch you in love and companionship.** When the moment is right, it is healthy to touch and be touched in love and affection. Positive touching is necessary for individual well-being and relationship health.

For example: John and Tina kiss before leaving for work. In this small way, they renew their connection.

This is respect.

Violence and assault or threats of violence and assault are wrong, disrespectful and a clear indicator of abuse

No one should have to live in a home where they need to be concerned about being hurt. Physical assault includes pushing, slapping, hitting, and throwing things.

No one has a right to make physical contact with you in an aggressive and hostile way.

For example: When Mark was upset with his wife Sally, he would move directly into her personal space, lock his eyes on her and raise his fist threatening to strike her. This is emotional abuse. Should he actually strike her, this is domestic violence. *This is disrespect.*

6. **To acknowledge your needs.** Part of a healthy relationship is acknowledging that both you and your partner have needs and that each of you should support each other in acquiring what you want. Hopefully, your partner understands this and respects

this fundamental relationship principle.

For example: Mary got an inheritance from her grandmother upon her passing. She asked her husband Adam what he thought was the best thing to do with the unexpected money. Adam felt respected. *This is respect.*

If your partner attempts to dominate you and does not consider your needs — this is disrespect and if it happens often it is emotional abuse

You have reasonable wants and needs. It may be something simple like a new pair of shoes for the holidays. If your husband or wife consistently refuses to acknowledge that what you want is of any importance, this is a sign of emotional abuse.

For example: Tina was going to the wedding of her sister. It was important to her to be dressed appropriately for the occasion. However, her husband Sam insisted that she wear an old dress and he refused to give her money for a new one. *This is disrespect.*

7. **To acknowledge your presence — this is respect.** People choose to be in an intimate

relationship — they are not forced. They believed their lives will be enriched because of this decision to live together. A basic ingredient of a healthy marriage is acknowledging the presence and value of one another.

For example: When Alona and Mark speak they look each other in the eyes. They acknowledge each other's presence. *This is respect.*

To be ignored or shunned — this is disrespect and if it happens often it is emotional abuse.

If your partner refuses to acknowledge your presence, this is a sign that something is seriously wrong in your relationship. If you ask your partner what is the problem and he or she will not tell you or is unwilling the work with you to solve it, this is a sign of emotional abuse.

For example: Sari is so mad at her husband Philip, she ignores everything he says. This has been going on for many weeks. Philip asks Sari what is upsetting her, but true to form she just turns away ignoring him. *This is disrespect.*

8. To be spoken to sincerely and gently. The primary

connection two people have with each other comes via talking. If you are sharing a life with someone, you have a right be spoken to with sensitivity and honesty.

For example, Eric is a construction site foreman and he typically speaks loudly and directly to the workers he manages. At home, when he speaks to his wife Cindy, he lowers his voice and speaks gently so she feels respected and cared for. *This is respect.*

Being spoken to harshly, insulted, called names or cursed — this is disrespect and if it happens often it is emotional abuse

If your partner repeatedly speaks to you in a harsh way, this is disrespect. Certainly, there will be moments when anger is expressed and harsh words may be said. Emotional abuse is determined when this type of treatment is ongoing and unrelenting.

For example: Frank tells his wife she is "ugly" and that no man would ever want her. He tells her that if she dies along with her mother, the world would be a better place to live. *This is disrespect.*

9. **To be honest, upfront and transparent.** You are

sharing a life with your partner. You have every right to know what is going on in your partner's life. When he or she shares with you the significant events that are happening in his or her life, this is respect.

For example, Matthew was asked by his boss to go on a business trip out of town. He discussed the matter with this wife Sharon and answered any questions she might have. *This is respect.*

To have secrets from you — this is disrespect and if it happens often, it is emotional abuse

If your husband or wife lives a private life and refuses to answer your questions regarding where he or she has been or worse lies to you about his or her whereabouts, this is emotional abuse.

For example: Bob never tells his wife Sarah when he is coming home or when he is leaving. He tells her she is not his mother and that he doesn't need to report to her. *This is disrespect.*

10. **To be mindful of your honor, especially in the presence of others.** Your partner should seek to honor you as he or she would honor himself or herself. This means not to criticize you before others

or say anything that embarrasses you. When your partner treats you this way, this is respect.

For example, when Brenda and Peter are in social settings, each is very careful to only praise each one another in the presence of others. Each feels respected by his or her partner. *This is respect.*

To intentionally embarrass you — this is disrespect and if it happens often it is emotional abuse

If your partner says things, especially in the presence of others, that are embarrassing or shame you, this is disrespect. If it happens frequently this is a form of emotional abuse.

For example: Karen is very open! She has no problem telling others that her husband Jack was fired from his third job in two years. How much of her private life she reveals depends on whether Jack is present. When he is with her, "She tells all!" *This is disrespect.*

The above descriptions and examples are to give you a clear understanding of what is abuse. These descriptions cover general areas. However, there are many relationship interactions that may not be listed here that are also abusive.

If you feel disrespected, put down, and devalued —
and this happens consistently — then these feelings
are likely the result of you being a victim of emotional
abuse.

If you do not feel good when you are around your life
partner, these feelings may be telling you there is
something seriously wrong in your relationship with
this person. Pay attention to your feelings! They may
be informing you that you are being abused.

There is no compromise! You are entitled to respect
so don't settle for anything less. This is your life and
you need to take care of it.

Fact #10. Emotional abusers can change — The 5 beliefs a reformed abuser must have and the 8 Relationship Guidelines for Past Abusers

Lisa is concerned about her future. Her husband Eric is always angry, yelling at her and at the children. When disappointed or annoyed, his anger and condemnation know no limits. He threatens her with divorce and says he will take the kids away. Being around him feels bad.

Lisa wants to know if her emotionally abusive husband can change? Can Eric become a better person and learn how to be a respectful and calm man.

Lisa comes from a divorced family. Knowing first-hand how hard divorce is for everyone in the family, she wants if possible to avoid it.

The simple answer to Lisa's question regarding, "Can

abusers can change for the better" is "yes."

In most cases, people who abuse others either have low self-esteem or have grown-up in homes where emotional abuse was present.

Both situations — low self-esteem and bad role modeling from parents — can be corrected and overcome and the abuser can change into a good person. However, this can only happen if the abusive person WANTS TO CHANGE.

If an abusive person 'does not want to change,' there is very little you can do. Depending on the level of abuse — and it is different in every marriage and committed relationship — you can either find relationship strategies to manage and cope with the abuse in a way that it does not injure you and your children (which is often impossible) or you can exit the relationship and break-free completely.

How do emotional abusers fix themselves and their damaged relationships?

Positive change is possible for everyone. Just as we can learn how to drive a new car or how to use a new computer program, so too someone can *change* an old set of behavior for a new one.

As a marriage and family therapist, I have witnessed countless men and women eliminate their abusive behavior and become kind, sensitive, and caring. However, achieving this success takes a lot of work by everyone involved.

Breaking it down, the following 5 beliefs and attitudes must be present in abundance if an emotional abuser is to change successfully and permanently. The more these traits are in abundance, the more likely positive change will happen. Without any one of the following this 5 beliefs and attitudes, the likelihood of positive change is significantly reduced.

The 5 beliefs a reformed abuser must have

1. **Objectivity.** If an abuser is to change, he or she must be able to recognize that he or she is behaving badly. The starting point of all self-improvement requires recognizing that one can do better. Within a relationship, learning how to behave better requires the ability to distinguish between one's behavior and the behavior of one's partner. Identifying that one's

behavior is the source of at least part of the problem — and perhaps the entire problem — is the act of being objective.

2. **Responsibility.** The abusive person must accept responsibility for his or her behavior. In other words, he or she cannot blame his or her partner for the ALL the bad behavior. Taking responsibility means showing remorse for past behavior and a willingness to find ways to prevent the bad behavior from happening again in the future.

Once responsibility is accepted, then a decision can be made regarding how to change the bad behavior for the better. If there is no acceptance of responsibility, then there will only be blame, avoidance, and no positive change will be possible.

3. **Humility.** Humility is an essential ingredient if an abuser is to change. Humility is like grease between two gears. Humility gives the abuser the strengths of character to say," I am wrong and I am sorry." Humility leads to remorse for having hurt his life partner and other family members.

The opposite of humility is arrogance and stubborn

defiance. If the abuser puts forth those bad character traits, he or she will never change.

4. **Self-discipline.** If the abuser gets to the point where he or she has decided to make positive changes in his or her behavior for the benefit of the relationship, he or she needs to carefully monitor how he or she speaks and behaves. The person engaged in self-improvement needs to have appropriate expectations regarding his or her entitlements. Achieving self-improvement requires an abundance of self-monitoring and self-discipline.

5. **Motivation.** Your abusive partner may have many of the above positive traits. However, this is not enough. Your partner needs to be sufficiently motivated to want to put-it-all-together. He or she must want a healthy and happy marriage or committed relationship. And your partner must be prepared to sacrifice his or her impulsive wants to achieve these relationship goals.

You and your partner must accept that eliminating emotional abuse and living peacefully and respectfully together is the best for each of you. This truth is highlighted especially if you have children.

Children do not do well with separation, divorce, and often remarriage. Knowing this will motivate both of you to do your part to overcome the abuse and reestablish trust and closeness.

As the abused person — you must not accept abuse and if appropriate give your abuser the chance to change for the better. As the abuser — you must acquire the above attitudes and behaviors that bode well for the future.

Yes, you can eliminate emotional abuse; emotional abusers can — and often do — change for the better. Successfully doing so requires the above five positive character traits: Objectivity, Responsibility, Humility, Self-discipline, and Motivation. There can be no compromises. This is the relationship "medicine" needed for a cure. Anything less will not work!

Emotional abuse is a deadly relationship disease. Fortunately, it can be cured. However, this is true ONLY when the abusive person 'wants to change.' And if he or she does, then it is usually worth giving him or her a chance to do so.

Often the help of a trained and competent

professional relationship specialist is necessary to ensure the abuse is completely eliminated and the past damaged has been addressed and overcome. This is not an easy task, and this highlights why abuse should be dealt with as soon as it starts so any potential damage is mitigated and reduced.

The following is a message for your abusive partner if he or she desires to fix the relationship damage he or she had done and contribute to your healing

If you feel your partner is interested in denouncing his or her past abuse, you can give him or her my **8 Relationship Guidelines for Past Abusers**. Depending on the device you are using to read this book, you may be able to copy the **8 Relationship Guidelines for Past Abusers** and send them to him or her.

The **8 Relationship Guidelines for Past Abusers** is a relationship map to guide your partner to transform his or her cruelty to kindness, love, and sensitivity and contribute to the rebuilding of your relationship.

8 Relationship Guidelines for Past Abusers

Hi, this is Marriage and Family therapist Abe Kass.

If you acknowledge that in the past you have behaved badly with your partner, I encourage to use my **8 Relationship Guidelines for Past Abusers** to reform yourself and contribute to your partner's healing.

At this point in time, you may be feeling ashamed of yourself, fearful about your future, and not sure how to undo the mess you have created.

Know YOU CAN FIX YOUR RELATIONSHIP... and contribute to your partner's healing.

Know that emotional abuse recovery is a process. Just like any type of healing, it takes time and effort. Don't rush it!

Perhaps your partner is threatening to leave you or has already left, and you want to get him or her back. The only way you can achieve this is if you acknowledge your bad behavior, your abusive behavior, and work through it with your partner so he

72

or she can begin to trust you and feel safe around you once again.

Typically, individuals who abuse others either have low self-esteem, or as children grew up in homes where emotional abuse was present, or if you are a man you were taught that men have the right to control women.

If any of this is true for you, you certainly CAN change for the better. There are ways you can find to improve your self-esteem, to educate yourself, so you know how to treat your partner with respect, and to accept that men and women are equal in value.

As we discuss this matter, I am going to assume three things:

1. *You have abused your partner in the past.*

2. *You are a "good" person, but you never learned the 'how and why' to treat your partner with respect.*

3. *You seriously want to change for the better.*

If these three points apply to you, then the following **8 Relationship Guidelines for Past Abusers** will help you clean up the 'relationship mess' you have made and reduce the likelihood that your abusive behavior will return in the future:

1. **Education.** Unless you know what emotional abuse is, it will be impossible to stop this bad behavior. Thus, your first task is to learn what in fact is emotional abuse. When you know what emotional abuse is, only then can you stop it! For example, sustained anger, ignoring, name-calling, threats, curses and more are all examples of emotional abuse. Not all relationship fighting is abuse. You need to learn what abuse is and what is not.

2. **Responsibility.** An essential component of emotional abuse recovery is taking responsibility for the abuse you have perpetrated upon your partner. In other words, you have no one to blame for your bad behavior accept yourself. You need to accept this fact, or you will never stop your abusive ways. If you blame someone else for your "bad behavior," what you are saying is that another person is controlling you — they determine your behavior. If this is what you believe, this means you can't control yourself — that YOUR behavior — good or bad — is dependent upon someone else. If so, how then can you ever

stop future abuse? Obviously, this is an unacceptable position, and you will fail in your efforts to stop abuse in the future and heal yourself and your partner from the past abuse. Verbalize to your partner — the victim of your abuse — that what you did was hurtful and wrong, that you are at fault and no one else, and you will make every effort to make sure it does not happen again. This is what it means to take responsibility for your past bad behavior.

3. **Humility.** Recovering from emotional abuse requires humility. You need to listen and understand how your abuse devastated your partner. When humble you can be empathetic, understand your partner's pain, and have the possibility to reconnect as a couple. Let your partner describe in detail his or her feelings without becoming defensive. Don't explain yourself, justify what you have done, point out inconsistencies, or hypocrisies regarding your partner's point of view and feelings. In fact, unless you are asked, "don't give your opinion at all." Just listen, listen, listen...

4. **Be patient.** Healing from injuries, be they physical or emotional, have their own timeline. You need to let your partner decide when and how the work on

recovering from emotional abuse is to happen. He or she may get over their injuries quickly, or it may take a long time. You should be prepared for either and adjust appropriately. Willingly hang in there as long as it takes. Let your partner decide when to "close the book" on the abuse.

5. **Self-examination.** Examine yourself to learn the sources of your abusive behavior.Knowing why you have behaved abusively in the past will help you understand your feelings and will help you take appropriate steps to make sure your bad behavior does not return in the future. If you do not know where in your life "your abuse" has come from, stopping your bad behavior will be more difficult. Like leaking water, if you don't know the source of the leak is, how then can you stop it? Ask yourself the question: Why have I abused my partner? Make sure you answer this question. This is an essential part of the healing process.

6. **Feedback.** Ask your partner to help you monitor your behavior and to let you know 'if and when' your behavior feels controlling, intimidating, and unreasonable. Be calm and appreciative when your partner gives you feedback letting you know that he

or she is uncomfortable with your behavior. This feedback must be used to refine your behavior making it more loving, kind, and respectful. Your partner's perception is what matters. It does not matter whether or not you feel you are "controlling, mean, threatening." It's how your partner EXPERIENCES YOU that matters. Perception is everything! If your partner says your behavior is bad, "accept" his or her words and improve your self.

7. **Forgiveness.** After you have spent some time working on taking responsibility for having abused your partner, and you have shown remorse and committed to not letting abuse happen in the future, you can then ask your partner to forgive you. Should your partner be gracious and forgive, be grateful. If you are not forgiven, humbly accept your fate without protest. You can always ask again for forgiveness at another time. Forgiveness cannot be forced. Genuine forgiveness requires your partner feel in his or her heart that you have made amends and it will not happen again in the future. Because forgiveness is a feeling and cannot be forced, the feeling of forgiveness must come naturally. However, how you behave during the recovery period will greatly

influence whether or not, in the end, you will be genuinely forgiven. Follow carefully The 8 Relationship Guidelines for Past Abusers and you increase the likelihood that your partner will eventually forgive you.

8. **Grateful.** Be grateful the victim of your emotional abuse is giving you a second chance. He or she is not obligated to do so. And when he or she does give you a "second chance," be grateful and know that a terrible fate for you and your family has been avoided. Verbalize your gratitude. Your partner needs to hear with his or her ears your sincere feelings of regret for the hurt you have caused and your appreciation that you have been given an opportunity to correct the bad behavior you had in the past. Emotional abuse is a deadly relationship disease. Many families are torn apart because of emotional abuse.

Unlike many serious medical conditions, emotional abuse can be cured. However, it is up to you — *YOU are the relationship doctor!*

Use these **8 Relationship Guidelines for Past Abusers** as a map to heal yourself and everyone injured by your past abuse.

Be a Marriage Builder, fix past mistakes and make for yourself and your loved ones a healthy relationship future.

Fact #11. Violence is a dangerous type of abuse

Although this book is about "emotional abuse," domestic abuse and physical abuse must be addressed. Often, emotional abuse can deliberately or accidentally slip into physical abuse. Because of the severity of domestic violence — someone can be killed — I would be amiss not taking some time to talk about it.

All violence between human beings is abhorrent. When violence exists between a husband and wife, between two individuals committed to sharing a life together, it is absolutely abhorrent.

Sadly, thousands of people each year are murdered and injured because of domestic violence. Typically, women are more often the victims of physical abuse since men are usually stronger and more physically aggressive.

Domestic violence and physical abuse includes pushing, slapping, assaulting with objects, punching, confining and throwing things. Some abusers are innovative and find cruel and unusual ways to torment their victims. All of this is deadly abuse and cannot be tolerated by the individual, the family, or the community.

Should your relationship become violent, you can never know in advance how it will end. Because of this, if there is violence in your relationship you need to separate from your partner immediately since one false calculation regarding the violence and how it will end, can lead to a situation in which there is injury and perhaps no return.

Sadly, in my work as a social worker doing forensic investigations, I have met men in prisons who have killed their partners. If there is violence, separate, get away from your partner... *don't take chances.*

If you are in a situation that could lead to physical violence, it is essential that you contact the police, doctors, professional mental health professionals, children's aid societies, women's shelters, family members and friends to help you and your children get to a safe place. *If you take the first step, others will come to your aid.*

Creating safety

If you are injured by acts of violence and aggression, you must protect yourself from additional injury. This requires the immediate elimination of all threats and acts of violence.

The means to this end is different for each person. Call the police if you feel your well-being is threatened. The police will intervene to makes sure you are physically safe. If your safety can be assured, consider relationship and / or anger management therapy.

If you suffer from systemic domestic abuse in any form, you need to take a look at the big picture and work out what your best options are. Speaking with a trained relationship specialists is advised to help you understand clearly what has happened to you and what may happen to you in the future if you do nothing.

Safety may be achieved by the violent person committing himself or herself to self-control and refraining from any additional violence, aggression, and extreme expressions of anger. If this is not possible, or even doubtful, physical separation is necessary.

Anger management therapies for the violent partner may be helpful. However, this may take months to complete and they may not even work. During this time, victims of assault cannot and should not be furthered injured waiting for the abuser to "change." The safety of all involved is the overriding criteria that must be used to determine the best way to proceed.

After your safety has been established, it may be possible to recover if desired from past injury and injustice by reconciling and establishing a healthy and respectful relationship. Help from a competent professional relationship specialist is essential.

People can and do change — but not always. It is your choice to attempt reconciliation when the physical abuse has stopped, but be prepared to end the relationship if the abuse resumes.

Safety-plan

If you are in a situation where your safety is uncertain or is threatened, you need to get immediate help.

Reach out to others and together develop a "safety-plan" to help you protect yourself and your loved ones. The details of your "safety-plan" will be customized to your particular situation and resources available. You need to seek out the appropriate authorities and professionals to help you put together your safety-plan.

Your safety-plan should include access to money, alternative housing, transportation, privacy, counseling and legal counsel to protect you from future violence or even the threats of violence. If you have children, there will be many details to consider. It is best to do all of this when things are relatively calm and you are not in a crisis.

Do not accept violence. Doing so is risky and even if you physically survive, the emotional wounds will be next to impossible to overcome even if the violence stops. If domestic violence becomes commonplace in your relationship, your marriage, and even your life, may have no future!

There should be a zero tolerance for domestic violence — both you and your partner should agree with this.

Fact #12. You need to take the 'right' action to end the abuse

If you live with emotional abuse, likely you have struggled with what to do about it. You wonder, should I stay or should I leave? The outcome of your decision will impact your entire life and if you have children their lives as well. For many, the decision impacts your life for years. There is a lot to think about when making this decision to stay together or break apart.

You must be safe

When deciding whether to stay in an abusive situation or leave it is essential that you evaluate your safety. You should not live in a situation that is physically unsafe and/or emotionally harmful. This is especially true if there is no hope positive change will eventually occur.

In particular, physical abuse can lead to a situation where there is no recovery. Somebody may be injured or even killed. You can't take your chance and if this is your situation you need immediate relief. Your abusive partner needs to leave, and if he won't, then you should leave — plain and simple!

If your conclusion is, perhaps after consulting with friends or professionals, that the emotional abuse can be significantly reduced or stopped, you may choose to continue until things eventually improve.

Make sure your children are okay

Certainly, if your children are being injured because they are either exposed to emotional abuse, or they are being abused, then you need to do something sufficient to protect them.

Certainly, a divorce will be difficult for your children and likely take a toll on their well-being... *however so will abuse, which is likely worse!*

Often when the abuse and conflict are chronic and out in the open, children are "relieved" when their parents separate.

Of course, divorce leads to shared custody, loss of financial resources, and the attention of two loving parents and is not easy to adjust to. However, making your children victims of secondhand abuse (abuse that is not directed at them), like secondhand smoke, should not be an option.

If your children are being hit, put down, threatened, enslaved — then you need to take immediate action to end the abuse. It is your responsibility as the non-abusing parent to protect your children!

If you and your partner do not have children, it is much easier and simpler to 'quit and start over' with a new relationship.

Before you make your finial decision to continue in your relationship or end it, It is smart to get professional help to assist you in making your final decision regarding how best to protect yourself, and if you have children, them too. *It is best to seek help from a professionally trained and certified marriage and family therapist and a family law lawyer.*

The positives of staying

Certainly, at one time you and your partner were very attracted to each other. Most likely, you even loved one another. There can always be a reasonable hope that with the appropriate efforts made you can return to this positive relationship place.

However, getting back to that loving place is only possible if you stay together. Separating rarely improves a marriage. Typically, the 'separated couple' becomes further polarized and mistrustful when living apart.

If you and your partner stay together, there is always the hope that things can get better and divorce avoided. Avoiding divorce is no small matter. For most, divorce is painful, disappointing and impoverishing.

The negatives of staying

Living in an emotionally abusive situation is injurious. Abuse will erode your self-esteem, sense of self-worth, and likely leave you anxious and depressed.

If you remain in the emotionally abusive relationship and you cannot see things improving in the near

future, you risk many types of physical and emotional injuries.

It may be difficult to envision a better life without your partner even though he or she behaves abusively, but it is possible to go on and have a better life with or without someone else. Freedom and safety — impossible when you are being abused — is a great tonic for your soul!

A book cannot be written as a whole — rather it needs to be written one page at a time. So too, when making dramatic changes to your life, you need to go one step at a time. Only in this way can the changes your are thinking about be carefully considered and then hopefully when implemented, they will lead to the desired outcome.

Fact #13. You must protect yourself from injury when in the presence of your abuser

If you are being emotionally abused and after careful evaluation of your situation you have decided to stay, you need to do something to stop the abuse. Some of the things to consider are as follows:

Know how to handle an abuser

Until you have stopped or significantly reduced the emotional abuse, you need to have industrial strength relationship skills to stay on top of the situation.

Read books, get professional help and learn how to take care of yourself .

Learn to let the emotional abuse be like water off a duck's back — try to not to let the abuse impact on you. Yes, this is easier said than done. However, if you have chosen to stay in your relationship until the abuse stops, this is your only reasonable option.

Remember, it is your choice to stay in your marriage

or committed relationship. Take responsibility for this decision. Doing so will strengthen and empower you!

For example, if your abuser calls you names, don't take it personally. His or her name calling is a reflection of his or her emotional illness and in truth has nothing to do with you.

Every person — you and your partner included —is unique. So too, your relationship dynamics are unique. Thus, it is impossible to give you specific advice. If you need help, consult an appropriate professional.

Overcoming destructive patterns

If because of the abuse in the past you have conditioned yourself to be passive or excessively compliant, you need to learn how to be assertive. Perhaps you have thought of yourself as less than worthy in your relationship. If so, you need to change this perception.

There are possibly many dysfunctional patterns of thinking that may have developed and taken hold within your mind as a result of living with abuse for years. These dysfunctional ways of thinking need to be identified and replaced with healthy patterns of self-thought and relationship interactions.

The following are a list of essential skills needed for healthy self-esteem and healthy relationship living:

- Thinking positively about yourself

- Know how to be assertive

- Know how to identify abusive behavior

- Know how to protect yourself when your partner is abusive

- Figure out how to get your reasonable needs met even if your partner opposes you

- Know how to live without fear of what your abusive partner will do

- Identify strategies you can use to live with hope

- Take a firm stand that abuse is not okay and find ways to help your partner become a decent human being that is respectable, kind and loving.

Living in an emotionally abusive situation, even temporarily, is high-maintenance and emotionally stressful. Remember, it is YOUR CHOICE to stay together and accept the responsibility required to make your decision a good one that leads to a positive outcome.

Heal yourself

If you are like most people who have lived in an emotionally abusive relationship, you have been emotionally injured... *and now you need to heal yourself.*

The nature of your injuries are likely unique because of your personality, past, and current relationship. If you need professional help to recover, then get it.

You need to get to a point in your personal life where you feel good about yourself, you understand what has happened to you in the past, and you are hopeful for the future. These are reasonable expectations that you should have for yourself, and you need to work hard and with dedication to achieving them.

You were born to be happy — claim your birthright. Don't let your abuse take you down. Rather, let it be a springboard to grow stronger, healthier, and happier.

Fact #14. You need to stop being abused — The 14 guidelines to a strong stand against abuse

The 14 guidelines to taking a strong stand against abuse

1. Make a decision for yourself and take a firm stand that you will not allow your partner to humiliate, shame, degrade, curse or threaten you.

2. Make a decision for yourself and take a firm stand that you will not allow your partner to intimidate, control or force you to do something you don't want to do.

3. Make a decision for yourself and take a firm stand that you will not allow your partner to trivialize your feelings, ideas, or values.

4. 'Silent treatment' emotional abuse is an act of

hostility. Make a decision for yourself and take a firm stand not to accept such treatment from your partner.

5. Make a decision for yourself and take a firm stand that you will not surrender your independence and autonomy by submitting to your partner's will.

6. Make a decision for yourself and take a firm stand to not accept extreme selfishness from your partner to the point where it is dismissive of your needs and wants.

7. Make a decision for yourself and take a firm stand that you will not allow your partner to isolate you from family or friends.

8. Make a decision for yourself and take a firm stand that you will not allow your partner to withhold money, confiscate your personal belongings such as car keys, your phone, or other personal property. Do not get into a physical altercation to prevent your partner from getting your belongings. Rather, look for a solution that removes you or protects you from this situation.

9. Make a decision for yourself and take a firm stand that you will not allow your partner to touch you in a

hostile way or to threaten to do so by making his hand into a fist, or getting very close to your face with his face, or any other menacing and threatening way.

10. Make a decision for yourself and take a firm stand that you will not allow your partner to behave in an extremely jealous and possessive way that impacts on your peace of mind, challenges your dignity, and restricts your freedom.

11. Get outside help if you need it. DON'T REMAIN SILENT. This is what your abuser wants you to do! Don't cooperate and unintentionally allow the abuse to continue his or her abusive behavior! Best to rely on a trained relationship specialist to get the relationship help you need. One good place to locate a trained and certified relationship specialist is: American Association for Marriage and Family Therapy [http://www.aamft.org/iMIS15/AAMFT/]

12. Recognize that you do not need to live as an abused person. If you want, you can leave your abusive partner. If you decide to leave, get help if needed to ensure your safety as you tell your partner of your plans or as you organize and implement your exit. Family and friends can help. The police are

available to ensure your safety. In some situations, it is advisable to consult a family law lawyer.

Professional help

Marriage and couples therapy can be very helpful, provided you find the right therapist. With the right therapeutic help even seemingly insurmountable problems can be overcome.

Most ordinarily trained psychologists, psychiatrists, and social workers do not have the specialized training required for solving complex relationships problems. Finding the right therapist begins with finding a therapist who is trained and certified to work with relationships.

Look for a therapist, psychologist, psychiatrist, cleric or social worker who can show you upon your request his or her specialized training and certification in relationship problem solving that prove his or her competence.

Unfortunately, many well intending professionals have made situations worse because they have not fully mastered the skills needed to help with serious marriage problems.

It is also important that you find a relationship therapist who really cares about you and your family and is willing to dedicate himself or herself to improving your situation.

Having the right therapist can be a lifesaver. The therapist can build a relationship with your abusive partner and explain to him or her how there is no advantage to continuing to be abusive and what the advantages are in learning how to treat you with respect, kindness, and consideration.

If you need a therapist to help you recover your self-esteem you do not necessarily need a relationship specialist. A caring, competent and licensed psychologist, counselor, or social worker is well trained to help you achieve this goal.

We all know the value utilizing the services of doctors, dentists, lawyers or accountants when necessary. So too, you should recognize the value in using a relationship specialist to help you with your serious relationship problems and emotional injuries.

Get the help you need to build, together with your

partner a healthy, happy and lasting relationship.

If money is an issue, you can always get self-help materials. However, taking out an additional credit card, as you would for a luxury vacation once every few years, is certainly reasonable to save your family, reduce your emotional pain, and protect your mental health.

A few thousand dollars of debt is easily justified if it prevents years of misery either living with an abusive person or living alone or perhaps entering into another relationship that will likely have its own set of problems.

If you have children, remarriage will likely be difficult for them and leave them at risk for emotional, behavioral and educational problems. Solving the problems between you and your partner would be the ideal solution for everyone, especially your children.

Relationship specialists are the best people to help you resolve abuse when are in a safe situation. Here are two of the best places to find these professional specialists:

In the USA: American Association For Marriage and Family Therapy

In Canada: Canadian Association for Marriage and Family Therapy

True, a good relationship specialist costs money. However, getting relationship therapy with the right person is likely the best financial investment you will ever make. Don't let money get in the way of living a healthy and happy life.

Fact #15. You need to preventing emotional abuse in the future

Should you stay in your current relationship, and the abuse has stopped, it is extremely important that you have a plan of what to do should emotional abuse return.

With your partner, discuss what the two of you will do if you sense the abuse returning. For example, if you have used the services of a competent therapist in the past, both agree if you are having problems in the future that you will return to him or her for additional help.

Self-improvement and relationship-improvement are rarely a straight trajectory. Typically there are many ups and downs, steps forward and then the occasional setback.

Successfully solving your emotional abuse problems and then having to return and deal with them again at some time in the future is not a failure — to some extent it should be anticipated. Relationship and personal problems, as physical ailments, should be accepted as a natural part of life.

Nothing comes easily, and this includes making a healthy and happy family.

Think of contributing to your family as an investment. Coupled with the "dividends" you will acquire from a healthy family — a meaningful life, a sense of belonging, purpose, celebratory moments — your family is your best investment. You can draw upon your relationship wealth throughout your life all the way to your old-age.

Individuals without family connections are sadly lonely and lost!

If you and your partner both agree that emotional abuse is unacceptable, then certainly you can keep it away. Should it unintentionally return, with a little tuneup, you and your partner can reestablish your fundamental relationship principals of love, care, sensitivity, and commitment.

Conclusion: Knowledge is power

The starting point for stopping an emotionally abusive relationship is being able to identify what is, in fact, emotional and psychological abuse and if these definitions describe your situation.

If you realize you are being emotionally abused, you are in a difficult situation. At the same time, there is an opportunity to make your relationship or at least your life better. There is hope!

You need to devise a practical plan to ensure your life now and in the future is a good one, a safe one. Don't accept any form of abuse — emotional, verbal, physical, sexual, or religious / doctrine.

Your partner does not have to like you. He or she does not have to spend time with you. The two of you may have arguments at times. And if it is like this, then you have marriage problems — and you should fix these relationship problems or you have the option to divorce. **However, your partner DOES NOT have a right to abuse you!** I hope from everything that has been said in this book is clear — *there is nothing you can do to justify your partner abusing you. NOTHING!*

However, relationship abuse is very different from relationship conflict and neglect. Your partner does not have a right to abuse and disrespect you regardless of how he or she feels about you.

Never accept abuse. Make the necessary changes to make sure all your relationships are healthy and you live with dignity, freedom, and respect. To succeed, the decision to act — to free yourself from relationship abuse — must be yours. No one will or can solve your problems unless you are a full participant!

If you are in an abusive relationship, take action NOW. Make a list of what you can do to stop the abuse and start going through the list now... one step at a time.

As well, positive change — eliminating emotional abuse — can take time. Victims of emotional abuse need to be patient and understand this.

Slow and steady progress towards a more respectful and harmonious life together as a husband and wife or as a committed partner is definitely worth the effort and time required. This is only true when the abuse does not include violence. If there is violence — hitting, pushing, etc. — you need to separate immediately from your abusive partner. The decision to return and live together should only be made after you are certain the violence will not reoccur.

You and everyone in your family is entitled to live a healthy and happy life. And to a great extent, this is dependent on having healthy relationships. There is no promise that getting to this utopian place, the peaceful and happy relationship, will be easy. However, happiness is your birthright... and you should claim your right to in a healthy marriage or committed relationship.

Remember, an "abuser" is a person, and as such, should he or she want, positive change is possible. Let your abuser know how you feel about his or her abusive behavior. If you feel unable to do this alone, for whatever reason, get another person to join you in this intervention. If possible, it is always best to give your abusive partner a chance to become better. However, if he or she won't — for whatever reason — likely it is best for you to get yourself, and if you have children, out of the abusive situation.

Whatever road you take to STOP the abuse, understand you can't know all the details of your journey with only your first few steps forward. Things will evolve overtime, and with careful planning, the right help, and blessings from Above, you will find your way to a better life — without a doubt!

No matter how difficult fixing your broken marriage or committed relationship may seem, never give up hope. Even small steps in the right direction will eventually add up and make significant positive changes for the better.

Wishing you and your family the very best,
Marriage and Family Therapist Abe Kass

Additional help

You can take our free Emotional Abuse Test and get an idea as to the severity of your current situation:

www.GoSmartLife.com/emotional-abuse-test

For additional relationship self-help tools and information go to:

www.GoSmartLife.com/marriage-intelligence-home

To learn more about our library of SmartLife self-help books and also our recommended books by other top professionals go to:

www.GoSmartLife.com

Leave a review on Amazon

Also important, you can help me and others by leaving a positive review if you think this guide warrants it.

When you do this, Amazon will promote this book and you will partner with me in helping others resolve their relationship challenges.

Thanks for your help.

More about Abe:

Abe Kass, M.A., R.S.W., R.M.F.T., is a registered Social Worker, registered Marriage and Family Therapist, certified Clinical Hypnotherapist, and award-winning educator and writer. He has a busy family therapy practice working with individuals, couples, and their families in Thornhill, Vaughan, Richmond Hill, North York in Ontario, Canada.

Abe is a member of the Ontario College of Social Workers, the Ontario and American Associations for Marriage and Family Therapy, and the National Board for Certified Clinical Hypnotherapists.

Abe is a graduate of Norwich University in Vermont, where he received his interdisciplinary master's degree in Social Work and Family Therapy. He also has a bachelor's degree in Psychology from the University of California where he graduated with honors. He successfully completed his internship at Jewish Family and Child Service in Toronto and the George Hull Center for Children and Families in Etobicoke. He is a former professor of psychology at the Beth Jacob Academy of Higher Learning in Toronto.

As an experienced registered Social Worker, registered Marriage and Family Therapist, and certified Clinical Hypnotherapist, Abe will provide you with a service of the highest quality and standard. Proof of the success of his work is that most of his new clients are referred to him by former satisfied clients.

Abe has worked for over 20-plus years helping couples and individuals living in Thornhill, Vaughan, Richmond Hill, and North York. As well, via Skype and phone he has counseled many individuals and couples throughout the world.

Besides finding a therapist that has the appropriate professional credentials — he or she must also have healthy personal values, and care about you and your family. Abe has all three qualifications — he has the highest professional credentials, healthy personal values, and he sincerely cares about his clients and their families.

At times, life can be very challenging for all of us. We can all occasionally benefit from the assistance of a teacher, coach, or guide during particularly difficult moments in life. Abe is ready to help.

Abe is married with seven children and is blessed with too many grandchildren to count. As well, he has four goldfish and one bullfrog in his backyard pond (at the time of this writing — the raccoon often unexpectedly changes these stats!)

Abe is a member in the following professional organization. This is proof he is the "real deal."

82033849R00069

Made in the USA
Lexington, KY
25 February 2018